W0115315

OSTINATO VAMPS

PITT POETRY SERIES

Ed Ochester, Editor

ALSO BY WANDA COLEMAN

Mad Dog Black Lady (1979)

Imagoes (1983)

Heavy Daughter Blues (1987)

A War of Eyes and Other Stories (1988)

The Dicksboro Hotel & Other Travels (1989)

African Sleeping Sickness (1990)

Hand Dance (1993)

American Sonnets (1994)

Native in a Strange Land: Trials & Tremors (1996)

Bathwater Wine (1998)

Mambo Hips & Make Believe: A Novel (1999)

Love-ins with Nietzsche: A Memoir (2000)

Mercurochrome (2001)

Wanda Coleman

OSTINATO VAMPS

POEMS

University of Pittsburgh Press

RED MOUNTAIN COLLEGE
LIBRARY
7110 E. McKELLIPS RD.
MESA, AZ 85215

The publication of this book is supported by grants from
the Pennsylvania Council on the Arts
and the California Arts Council.

Published by the University of Pittsburgh Press, Pittsburgh, Pa., 15260

Copyright © 2003, Wanda Coleman

All rights reserved

Manufactured in the United States of America

Printed on acid-free paper

10 9 8 7 6 5 4 3 2 1

ISBN 0-8229-5833-3

For my son, Baby Boy, Ian Wayne Grant

CONTENTS

I. Red Noir

II. Ostinato Vamps

III. Two Fugues & a Prayer

IV. The Weighing of My Heart

Under the bludgeonings of chance,
My head is bloody, but unbowed.

—William Ernest Henley

I.

RED NOIR

Revenants

under the dark gnarled word
the tongue moves slowly
brains Rex lard fried
yet realization comes quick
secrets seeded in relentless earth
womanly desire daring the solace of
      snake-eyed men
who break mulish hymen & spill
      cotton gin histories
hard on the looksee for rain & weevils

at the close of each pleasure's taking
they exchange smokes, brew, and quips
while the word moves slowly
works through topsoil to impregnate
unrest, shoots uncoiling like
the spent arms of contentious lovers

and the women plow the heart, pain-defiant
jaws locked against the law
counting the comings and goings of every
father, son, & so-and-so
waiting on word of deliverance

Yellowed Parchment

guarded like the gates of slave quarters
inscribed with delusions of freedom,
the desire for liberty molded into flesh,
time between bleedings lengthens.
women blossom with the unborn
held like secrets in the womb of history

millions vanish
from the text of the telling
their stories stolen and revised
to fit the narrow imprint
of plunderers and exploiters

conjure up Abyssinia and Alexandria, flood the
almighty Mississippi.
with purity comes pain
splendor is the dream fully realized
and in memory all ugliness restored

Nipples Like Thorns Piercing Thoughts

she does an intoxicating fade

a lover discovered entombed in warm stone
she presses her body against his back
the lost continent of his face carved with cheeks as broad as
        the centuries
full regal lips, the eyes of a jaguar. awakened,
he leaps from the cage of her hunger, breath at her throat
raising kink-down patch, racing the blood

the museum a jungle
the cry of Quetzalcoatl cross the river of nails

Relocation on the Edge

seven doors keep   their secrets   here
   a morning cool concealed   although there are no
locks or safes   spiders, dust, and tissue-thin desperation
   the electric heart   not my own ghost, but others
he is listening   as he does every night   at our keyhole
   to our heated sex   the living spectrum of ordinary
pretensions   this city of shames   day and night long
   glass hides nothing   lips swarm soundlessly
something races the room   like a mosquito
like a deathless beast   trapped   in an ancient dungeon
         like a tangled identity

78 rpms on a Piper's Dream

thin brown men in fedoras, noses around highballs
and high heels in
lowdown uptown waterholes
where heavy-hipped canaries in sequins and pearls
chirp blues amens

meanwhile, on screen there's mystery afoot

the manifestations of blackness everywhere
from trombones to vibraphones
but not a skin deeper than tan to be seen. this
is the segregated world of salt-toned hipsters
where greetings to alligators in spats 'n' porkpie hats
are prelude to the ritual of escaping the lash
of recognition—plenty to imbibe and a den of nasties
to get gone on between Tokyo Rose serenades

freedom is a blurred state of vision

frozen between frames, find the redcap
ushering swells to the dining car. hide
in his pocket where the change bojangles. go to
where he's whistling *Lover Man* as he climbs
into sportin' duds. run with the palm of his hand
along those pomade-slicked back naps. pick up
the grease of groove and slide into a half-pint
of bathtub rotgut. splash with the funk of his
sweat into that bearded smile. listen to the
tappity-tap of toes as he tamps crystal stairways
      to that wild-winged hebben

Wichita Down West Home

oath-free colored Oz-talk
about a little tail & a lot of trouble draws
the laughter of dusk-toned men over
red punch & lemonade, a card club kind
of wisdom & wisecracking
found in playrooms or off back stoops

still heat catches breeze as early evening
descends o'er trim lawns and pastel-hued A-frames

and their heavy-hipped women with
pressed hair & aprons
set out the fried chicken & potato salad,
the dirty rice & greens, peach cobbler
& cherry cherry pie
while dream-kissed teens test
foot-and-leg work to radio rhythm rock
and black-eyed tots hide & seek & all fall down

(in this golden state of California exile)

grace is said above lowered heads

this is how the spell works—something like
a rumored normal or legendary equality

something like pearls

Cold Meat & Three Empty Shells

1)

the gat-toting duchess, permanently minus the duke
is swathed in silver lamé, a once slender fox
with well-turned ankles, pallor defining forty years
of malignant neglect and shoulder-length bigotry
captured in pinstripes with a cinch at the waist

the naked camera reveals the absence
of a noir-skinned temptress, too erotic to be seen.
she slinks at the periphery of celluloid memory
like a spook-driven simoniac, seller of candles & clove

the street scene concluded, the set goes dark

like homing pigeons the dangerous dames return
to the back-lot casino where the essentials of life ride
the number 4 or red on the roulette table.
this is the realm of Marlowe & Spade,
where the clarinet sizzles as coupe doors slam, clues
lead in spirals and straight propositions are bent

where "ain't nuthin' funny" is the epitaph of a saint

2)

there's always a jazz band laying down jitter riffs
all two-toned and marcelled, swaying or jumping,
waiters as enigmatic as pharaohs, and wide-hipped
low-toned jungle babes burning down the palms

3)

just another movieland puss poised
at the rim of a highball glass, spinning lies off
thrill-hungry lips, moist and splashed in pricey cologne

kiss-riddled, he slumps facedown onto the mattress,
bleeding from every reel, scared and sore,
yet eager for the next smooch

these are lips that kill, lips braced for the info,
revealing, perhaps, the hint of a smirk with
smile potential. edgy lips, making involuntary kissy
motions, going through the O's
lust-bruised kissables giving into a tongue fuzz,
spite lips, like an equal sign, arcing to make
soft nibbles in the intimacy of a private dawn

have lips. will . . .

encompassing the unspeakable
working its way past the teeth

Lady Sings the Blues 1969

1)

i haven't been conceived yet
haven't been born
yet Lady Holiday is singing my blues
twenty-three years later here i am ears deep
into her song, notes burning in my soul
words decades old still too true, caught up
in the same ol' slavery/love-for-a-black-man slavery
get-up-in-the-morning-face-another-day slavery
cry-lonely-in-the-night slavery
listening while Lady swings my blues

burning out my soul
with old names for new tensions
can't pay the rhetoric tensions
dying in The Dream tensions
too-black-for-some-folk tensions
carry epithets in self-defense tensions

twenty-three years deep
into Lady Day wringing the white out my blue

2)

Lady knew about the jive-assed brothers together
with their "philosophy" the big-mouth the big word
the big-wow talking the cause sweet-tongued, zip-witted
zigzag B-bruthas all play all theater all curtain call & no cast party

Lady knew about the hours between gigs
when hunger is blues. the hours between lovings
when hunger is blues. the hours between laughs
trying to kick the ain't-shit blues,
going home to greet the dust and the echo of a life

i'm on my knees rocking
on the floor on my knees groaning on the floor
into the scratchy hi-fidelity
on my knees as i sing along
twenty-three years forever bluesing out my brown eyes

and i wonder as i romance the night
will i be unlucky and live tomorrow?

3)

autumn—not in New York—but in my heart
evergreens and rose-gold October sunsets

going to my head as the air blows in off the sea
Lady—no waterfronts, but cement & neon

care packages of sausages & chocolate,
love-stained letters to my man in Vietnam

autumn—not a leaf turning—but my hope
spinning fantasies from cobwebs & cracks

Lady—no waterfronts, but cement, neon & padlocks

4)

a turn for the blues, i am the sofa-bound odalisque
fending off the workday with a heavy dose
of moonlight chased by sparkling burgundy brew

essence of daze-eyed and haunted, heartbreak never
felt so luminously rendered—so regrettably wise

Thirty Seconds over America

it's all slop jars and kerosene
dirty skillets and moonshine jugs

legendary women with grazing mouths
scalding breasts hypnotizing tongues liquefying breaths
working nightshifts and making change
under the spell of knuckles

impressions of soul embedded in fragments of rhythm
the anguished moans of absentee lovers
every cell screaming
loud enough for the world to know

inspiration comes on the ghost
of a rhythm-soul chanteuse, as each note slips
off/that dues demon tune,
strong enough to peep a longing before
she's slumped over in a daze of hustle

professional sleepwalking
in the house of the priest
on hotbeds of racial strain

head rolling under the palms of hands, head all up
the frying pan, head lingering for the honey's flow

inebriated on immorality
the ever-fatherless babies running streets
like Sunday chasing Saturday

there's a rainbow over Ararat
painted in sunny yellows and aquamarines

Requiem for a Nest

the winged thang built her dream palace
amid the fine green eyes of a sheltering bough
she did not know it was urban turf
disguised as serenely delusionally rural
nor did she know the neighborhood was rife
with slant-mawed felines and those long-taloned
swoopers of prey. she was ignorant of the acidity & oil
that slowly polluted the earth, and was never
to detect the serpent coiled one strong limb below

following her nature she flitted and dove
for whatever blades twigs and mud
could be found under the humming blue
and created a hatchery for her spawn
not knowing all were doomed

Almost Pregnant

1)

wrapped in his drunkard's thickness/body
scars like half-smoked stogies. kisses
that reek of Seagram's and motor oil.
two hundred pounds of bone & bother.
hands i can't deny. married hands.
it's too much, that wet-on-wet—the
ultimate high of coming/copulation
and never coming down until completed,
even then an orgasmic floating follows
me into the week ahead. gauze-eyed. then,
a dumb girl's horror at the absence of my
bloodjet. caught! trapped up in his body,
too much jelly and not enough mercy.
clean panties and no cramps. on or off
rhythm—the ultimate price, conception.
the belly will rise and never come down
till a child is completed (i think)
ever after, then, a preworld floating
remembered vaguely as mama's unsteady
stroll, swollen with fear and confusion,
seeking saline shots and the red tide's return.

2)

innermost urgency, the haste
of hands spreading flesh, hands pulling
and pushing. heavy cotton. the history of our future
in the blood-soaked patch of black lamb's wool
between my beswaddled thighs

3)

his baby will not be a mulatto.
his baby will teethe on pig's feet & neck bones.

his baby will crack corn with jimmy.
his baby will be mama's maybe.
his baby will be blacker than Rodessa at noon.

4)

"if you are, please have it."

> his touch is naked, soul-searching
> but the ring he wears is not mine. he
> smells like denial and desperation.

"if you are, please have it."

> eyes like peach pits stare up at me
> from my bed, trace colors and shapes,
> half-beg, half-threaten.

"if you're pregnant, please have my baby."

> it seemed he spoke a mighty
> recitation of ancient exultations
> to the unholy, road-dog incantations
> of back-alley angels and dumpster rats.

5)

i stumble into the infinite embrace
reach back to free myself—a tangle
of blood-pressure cuffs, tongs, and stirrups

i stumble.

carved on my belly,
imprints of broken stars

Meanwhile in San Francisco

lone cold brings on chilblains
it's in the deep sixties and
this is the city of free love and paisley
hug-a-drug & eat-a-bug kulture

a sexual revolution going on as
panthers & peacocks mate to produce a movement

against dim desire he watches. i undress quickly
beneath the Dutch ceiling, slip out of pink panties.

he's already naked
with a nice hang
as thick as my fist
between powerful chunky legs
which makes up for his being two heads shorter,
his mouth barely at my nipples

"where are you from?" he asks
"south hell."
"are you married?"
"no, but involved."

we are young. we are ebony. in The Garden we rake the leaves

he grows sad. "i've never been married. women don't like
          short dark men."
the climb into his bed is a plunge into ice water. i shiver.
he hurries, places his body so we fit
"stay, please stay lady, whoever you be," he begs

i fail to explain, know i'll be gone come sunrise
i'm in love with a place, not a man

Art & Embellishment

this week i'm into curlicues,
hemolytic poisons, Scotch plaids, and
frou-frou on my gargoyles

i chase my bourbon with asti spumante
one can't have too much chrome
or too much landau on one's brougham

as we drive the shore in Bondi Beach
i bend to tie my orange shoelaces under
a tall pine in Griffith Park as the fey waiter
at Café Luna tells me they've changed the
menu and no longer serve my favorite panini
Paul says this is a bad scene and he can't
handle it man as i deplane in Honolulu
i'm overcome by foreboding & disappointment

when all my untold stories break for the exit
my head explodes

slavery's been dead nigh a century
or more but i carry my chain everywhere
i am a lower form of urban intelligence
traveling the backside of the underground
stranded where the cul-de-sac crosses
the dead end. it is 110° in the heat forever
and the concrete is boiling my feet inside
this gummy crust that used to be my sneakers

how many African violets does it take
to jump-start a heart?

Cool Cats Snap Spats

starched collars wilt under the solid
rain of nostalgia punctuated by soft brown eyes
jacked but brilliant but powerful but banished
to Sylmar while over the hill
Hollywood stunts under murky sunshine
where The Blue and The Gray still fight an uncivil war

make the early report
prison rope zonk dope tears mope
the wineglass holding his heart
black granite monoliths
rainy climes and emerald fish

the reflection of futuristic walls, pressing against
geometric lines
widening the window on hell

like torrential pain

dig, walking loose ground
like harvest of faith
dig—flirty, bought and sold in flesh units,
mental corrugations
witness the end of ramshackle sanities
inhabited by rats roaches and mosquitoes
a legacy of purple brown and ebony
the bitten bare feet of the young and fearful

take science with thy daily bread
collect abandoned mysteries

remember. escape is seasonal

Things Go Sour

1)

having trouble with doors. they don't open
or open too swiftly like trap doors in a marriage/the
wicked light that reveals that nothing hoped for
was hidden in those once dense shadows

the gent vanishes

night roils on like decaying celluloid in a forgotten canister
(that's the plan made to assassinate dictators of the eye,
never mind the heart)

2)

the last door leads to a deserted arena
where the fighter reels in the ring
under kliegs, to the jeers of one, hopes contact
will first shatter then seize consciousness
before the canvas comes up for a kiss

3)

the trouble is with doors that open onto graves
or prison courtyards

4)

there are no bleached blondes in this claustrophobic's
scenario, no flights to Rio to bask beachside
or sip dark rum punch under sun-blitzed umbrellas

the trail doubles back upon itself
our protagonist mute before that towering

and resolutely slammed door, poised there
in a rain of splinters,

a shadowy figure sliding to its knees

5)

door trouble. open sez me. someone holds the knob
from the other side

6)

recurrent dream: i run naked down a corridor of doors
breasts and bottom bouncing, feet kissing cold marble
all open instantly, lead to more doors
each corridor colder, each door more ornate

7)

before entering the library
stop a moment. think. there may be something
unknown hiding against the wall, behind the other side,
waiting for you
to present your back, revealed and vulnerable. and just
as you turn, just as you suspect you
are being observed,

it will spring and take possession

Red Noir

—*after a collage by Austin Straus*

the city closes around you
a pillow held down over your face
your hands grip that stranger's
as you struggle for air

you hear the heaviness of breath
        like stymied flappings of salted wings
you hear the distant laughter
        of neighbors made oblivious by baseball & beer
you hear the forlorn rumble along tracks of
        ghost trains to Chinatown

it is daylight but you are buried in darkness
seeing everything dimly, as if by neon

you feel eyes walking your skin
and know for certain that there's a witness
to your ambivalence, hidden in the shadows,
afraid to get involved

this is where you live, under the eaves
frequented by jilted lovers and petty thieves

you wear your loneliness like a trench coat
pull its collar high against the chill
as you walk the night whispers
along the back alleys of your soul

Red Eye & Black Beans

done et till ah cain't move. full to my big toes

arched feet beneath a full-grown stomach
laid back like minor tributary, skin aglow and sparking
red under the black

unseen, the Satyr's Moon beams—its one eye brightly
crossing that part of the dark sky seen cockeyed out
the half-opened window and dust-caked screen

voices softly moan the songs of young love
singing nastily of nasty things in strong reds and weak blacks

the red of tongues lickin' the black off her
she strokes the coils close to his scalp, his thick muscular
arms brewing the blood that will raise her belly

steeped in mellow red brew, the mood blacker than
licorice sticks

evenings of red sun and long black shadows fading
into cool breezes and bared thighs and breasts

the fresh smells of cut mango and too-ripe banana
(she was red on her father's side and her mother's,
but there was more than enough niggah to go around)

breaking head open, watch the red run until black.
when the clots appear, you'll know it's over

Los Angeles Nocturne

Eternity ends where Hollywood begins

to be THERE is to scarf and strangle
on those cool thick lids and hot brown eyes
is to possess the unpossessible/fever and cure
is to ignite those cold stars over Avalon
(like stumblers through long-unpaved hearts
looking for the back entrance to love)
is to set them in a dreamscape of asphalt & desire
a sea of tight ambition & loose thighs

southerly off Graham, streetlamps wave like raffia
when earth quakes. nightprowlers
cruise jungle to jungle, anxious to score the light

no reservations tonight. it's a dress-down affair

stilettos like high-pitched hopes heard
stabbing down sidewalks while
behind slammed doors the Molochs tally
ill-gotten dreams and low-hung coupes take
stops doin' the South Central Roll

the unreachable unbreachable unteachables
hands shoved so deep into pockets
they can feel the next world

>   remember the Parisian Room
>   remember the California Club
>   remember Memory Lane

Normandie zigs where Jefferson zags

(you too can touch it. as much
as you want
you too can taste it. as much
as you want

there is everything to feel. there. throbbings
in your palms like my heart)

Eternity ends where Hollywood begins

II.

OSTINATO VAMPS

Broken Rhythms

like spellstuff   all the conceits i have shed
collect   on sun-splashed soil   where a
three-headed woman gathers them to make
her hoodoo   a powder in fire   to summon a spirit
a finely ground pinch in alcohol   to cure
a cough, or in a salve   to beautify aging skin
make your wish   for love   for hate
and burn the fragrant wax with a hint of dust
chant   toward the sky   watch.   the children gather
watch the children   dance   watch the children's eyes
watch.   the children with tongues   like wolves

Jazz Theory 101

our best, as it seems, are some of many
we try to touch the soul,
but the soul changes course and it's difficult
to come up with new temptations
that would ordinarily promote movement,
as in side-to-side

slide trombone did you say? crazy ears
vibrant and progressive and wow
the desire to be rooted or rooting in

finding inspiration in the inspired
miles of minor chords and major truths

history emanates from art
like where would the military be without the march?
aesthetics is the science of vulnerability
bruises transformed, wounds immortalized

blow Joe blow
there is a ness for every random
gather up thy baggage
recreate the sounds of thy homeland
let your fingers taste the beauty
summon your loved ones to the temple
reveal the sweetest part of agony

Dream Fever

my windows are barred
against the intrusion of ghosts

those thieving contours that steal the night
the neighbor's dogs howl at the whiff of phantoms
like youths with nowhere to frazzle but parking lots
or corners
(nuthin' you can tell me
'bout hauntings i don't know.)

recant a heritage of spooks if you must.
opaque, they'll deflect vision, then
riding on a chill, will rob you of your heartbeat
untransformed by either love or wanton sex
those horror-house refugees, blazing bebop
and don'tchewknowdaddio
on the dull end of abandonment
spotted five-o until payday

the themes and motivations of our common despair

my mind is barred and bolted
to obstruct the justice-sucking haints and sleepbreakers
tender at the flanks of round brown,
horns thrusting, taloned appendages flying, fangs
that lengthen on doubt
creeping as easily as angelfeet
blowing Judas kisses to my soul

tonight they'll come, almost obscure, on the
hum and the buzz of disfigured hopes
reveal a life of abandoned closets, former occupants
seeping through the cracks in my cranium

tonight i'll sleep with both eyes open

Ostinato Vamp

i am the daughter of earthquakes
dissonant and disruptive in my reign over Deathland
                    i stole
from god-slinging hypocrites in chaps, chinos, & spurs
from the sacred tribe of water-headed satyrs
on an abstinence from abstinence binge, shysters given
judgeships, panderers governing media, sanctioned gamblers
sapping the strength of negrodocious communities—there's
the necessity of music cut with bloody weepings

i stole it because it was mine
doowopshewopdewop ohsocherry

as committed as murder, i am inspired by heavily
cologned and powdered harridans plum narcissistic
and brain-strained under kelly green neon in the
              throes of supremacy, making
white noise proclamations of inappropriate behavior
syndrome synonymous with and analogous to congenital
              boneheartedness

i stolt it back cuz twas mine from da get-go
brown thighs meeting white west of The Pacos

in our bed   my absence   whispers beneath   his weight

ready to fornicate /blindly penetrate
(a bad season spent chained to a filing cabinet
bosses like dogs barking for important files
the rain of empty talk riving the intellect—no place
to run. work—a necessity in these hind quarters)
              all shook up
a rumble mama burped and there i was. take
these rhythms as evidence, my splendid rock-and-roll

Plum Hunger

the last note finished
and left me empty
craving the night.
i play Strayhorn again.
let him take me coolly
by the ears and lead
me back through
those lofty moments
when the imagined is
as good as actuality
down to that tavern
where broad shoulders
are rubbed against the
cold. i play Strayhorn
again. and i'm in upper
town wherever, lit to
the gills on the thrill
of having my beauty
admired. i play that man
until the grooves begin
to deepen and the walls
quiver, air turning silver
and blue. and he's with
me dancing, that man
i've conjured up, with
broad shoulders and
the arrogance to match.
he's a spirited spinner
and in no time, we're
off to Strayhorn, laid in

Soul Traveler

not dispersing but containing blackness

it was the ending and so reruns began
Amazon style, summer came calling,
fried brains and all. dumbfounded
in Los Angeles where mosquitoes drowse
in noonday heat, bloodlust drained from
tropical eyes, the air thin as a haint's brassiere

luxmobiles took the heights like llamas
where dollars shine from foreheads as smooth
as polished fenders, and from oversized
designer pocketbooks toted under shaved
and flavored underarms, breasts revealed
in bright colors, tank tops and bustiers

negra Afro angel

pat those cheeks in Spanish,
those too round strutters—a lingo dug by all

quietly there's reciprocation in snatches
from whistling lips, sunbeams and posters of James Dean

(shy tourist girl, a face all acne and
inexperience, shares her mother's
private smile. "buy something, some trinket.
support the local economy")

the emissary from G.O.D. calls her over,
places the silver cross at her throat, fixes her
with agate eyes, fingers splayed against
her hips. she follows him to the other side

of the moon, counts the hours under azure,
feigns reachings for her pen

note: plastic trash bags, cheap jewelry, the ebony cat in the cradle

she is made of ocean spray,
condor feathers and memories of sin

Mahalia Jones

in a colored realm, the glory-breasted
        mother of a
potato-headed tot, the one with little kinky
        knots dotting
his scalp, puts on the Motorola and plays
        her morning's
uplift over mochajava at thirty-three rotations
        per minute to
wash away a multitude of sins hemming her in,
        to inspire
those sweet chariots coming forth as she wades
        deep river of
long nights when her honeysuckle james is
        out with his
lowlife cronies while she tends their bed and the
        church pews
alone o lord she trembles at her own toughness
        as she busts
the dust slavin' seven-to-four. if it weren't for
        Graham Bell
& Marconi, she'd lose her mind as well as that
        heavy heavy
load. bye and bye she wearies and stops spinning
        those long-playing
hopes, the inspiration dries up as the hours
        lengthen and
in her sunset, her manchild will steal them away
        to barter in
exchange for rent and a shot at his own promise
        while those
idiot saints go marchin' on in the wrong direction
        backwards

The Boys of Loco Heights

all crotch and attitude
they bustin' in and bustin' up.
beer for breakfast
dodgin' bullets in the afternoon,
(beer for lunch dinner and snacks)
life one big dogfight
and they're out for the final howl
the projects, naw—the incubator to them
apartments darker than midnight so black
the cracks in the walls can be felt
when not seen. Momma got a new lover/whop
upside the head. Momma got a spankin'
new bawler-and-crawler likely
to half starve before it's able to walk.
if it lives it will be set straight.
there's lots of rhyme and jive
to fill the space between smokes,
dalliances with youth authority grads
and girls with thighs that smell like woman
enough to roll with in the streets, a teen-aged
death squad driven drumblood by
the twisted tongue—sending old men
and A-students to early graves,
fillin' the abortion clinics and mortuaries.
they don't speak proper English
they don't speak proper Spanish
they won't speak unless given a reason
eyes darker than Azreal's balls
so black no one can see 'em crack

Fragments of an Essay

O Danny boy, the pipes of Pan are playing from sea
to sea and down the purple mountain's majesty . . .

August—the anniversary of a sadness that aroused
recent public outcry passed quietly, unnoticed

a teenager found suspended from a rope. no crusade
followed to outlaw the laws that perpetrated his poverty

(he wanted to save Mom the trouble. the other kids
needed her more. love's demand an extreme sacrifice)

no plaque in his name declaring this the day welfare
for the corporate rich ended, no press conference

a 13-year-old boy hung himself because Mom
worked and slaved but could not provide enough

among the lower classes, what's one more statistic
mobility upward or even sideways non-newsworthy

life complicated by miseducation, workplace
difficulties and four layers of law, no matter

impoverished children, well, they're just another
class of nigger like undocumented workers

how hard the struggle. too familiar a story:
growing futility, increased violence, fixed-income poor

below the poverty line . . . happiness that has a price
tag on it. retired seniors reentering job markets

consumer interest groups proselytize simple matters
food clothing shelter—losing those good old basics

used to be available jobs. ironically such stories still
very much what's current, an American preoccupation

the conscientious working Mom paying for crime, left
with all the responsibilities while Dad's incarcerated

one 1 3-year-old hung himself because Mom couldn't
provide food enough to feed them all in Dad's stead

he wanted her not to worry. being the de facto man
of the family, what could he do to save that family

when discussing democratic ideals vs. death economics
remember Danny Holley. he died for no good reason

*O Danny boy, the pipes of Pan are playing . . . from sea
to sea and down the purple mountain's majesty . . .*

Straight Out of Autumn

cautious feet pad the suburban road to Xanadu
suffer bent toes and appalling corns
the designer hills are bright with clover
and a rain-fresh wildness denies the shroud
(into a soft sadomasochism herself she wears
black and boas well, poses as a vamp)

at the end of the short rope
made over in Farmington but calls Hollywood home
all moans of empathy are fake and conceal
the long secret laughter of an ex-junkie gone tweeker

(she slashed a guy's tires once and they weren't
even lovers. she had another's mail rerouted,
and still another of her victims mysteriously
lost his job without ever knowing why)

not your Shakespearean kind of Kate
envy thrives on the pain of so-called friends

there will be no spring this year
an arctic summer on the breeze
blight will spoil the coming harvest of stars

      good thing

she feels parched without tears filling her teacup

Likes Tangerine Sushi

arch of eyebrow, crook of pinkie
pimp clothes dripping glitter gold
he's as sincere as salmon—dream suction
that reefer-lipped guerrilla
into fast-food romances with mango braise
and unadulterated ancient ingredients,
unsheathes nuclear fish

"better to be desired in hell than ignored in hebben"
he's fond of saying

the bone-cracking performance of lips
draws smoke rings from labia
a spectacular stroking but
how well does one do a life?

by any loving deemed necessary.

cup him where he curves

A Second Death

how many times did he manage to shred
her confidence on his tongue? how many times
did he beat her into the ambivalence of grabbing
a butcher's knife and taking it to his clothes?
how many times did he call her bitch
until the epithet grew teeth?

lightning-quick off the bay
thunderheads summon a ritual rattling
cause a chill to the weak pink marrow

an afternoon's unruffled sleep following sex
spurs her to resist a murderous urge

(at the restaurant they exchange rages.
she broadsides him with her blackened
Cajun chicken sandwich. he pierces her cheek
with a French fry. she anoints him with his freshly
poured glass of white Zinfandel and stomps out)

there's little time for fear and none for wonder
she determines to leave him
if for a deeper mystery
if for a sweeter silence, if for a deadlier smile

but once through the door, she circles the block
spins as all directions fuse
and the speedometer registers zero

nowhere to go and no one waiting
but him

After the Rampage

detect the bits of smashed beer bottles
husks of dreams and crushed expectations
triangular shadows leaning sunward

molecules of sweat and thatches of hair
flies and ants grasping what's edible as it rots
against the cement, under broken branches
bus benches overturned, lampposts busted

reconnect the severed wires that dangle
strangely on the acrid air. rebuild the ruined
territory formerly owned by dwellers on the edge
measure the prayers it will take to balance the fear

revisit the enthusiasm that once connected
meaningful to challenge. survey the ancient wisdom
reconfigure plate glass, twisted gropings
and burned-out intentions

apologies wishes regrets

Designer Bag and All

street crone hugged up
in her August overcoat
(as bright as nuclear
dawn over Hiroshima)
concealing the flab
or simply trying to melt it off
and wears a scarf
to keep that castaway wig
tied to her head (the color
of honey pot fuzz
or bitter lemon over ice)
sittin' squat in the middle
of the block against
the cement clutching
two drab-olive trash bags
like one contains
the Ark of the Covenant
and the other a full-length mink
(thoughts as dusty as Jemima
with a whiskbroom, brain as
wrecked as two trains running
head-on down the same track).
she got dirty feet peeking
through the gaps in her rubber
soles and works her toothless
hirsute jaw with permanent
hunger, the Styrofoam
sandwich box for offerings
where the coins and one
tortured Washington speak
loud enough so that she
doesn't have to say a beggar's
word (ask a dollar earn a dollar,

give a dollar earn a friend)
or explain that port wine stain
covering three-quarters
of her face. it's all been
said a hundred times before
to indifferent social workers
and callused police officers
(you can't judge the devil
by measuring the horns)
she no longer stinks because
the shit has dried onto her dignity
(going like stoned in the sixties,
as desolate as Love Field).
there was, indeed, a lover/
a romantic encounter, but
if he had loved her the way
summer loves the sun she
wouldn't be sittin' there now
smokin' her cigarette stub, blowin'
smoke rings and scratchin'
that tattoo above her crêpe paper
titty while pretending no one stares

moonsparkle angelsleep
mother hips
diamond dust
childworn
bless you

Translations from the Night

—after R. C. Glenn

Greasy wannabe longdong mofos

> the youngblood speaks his rage, encodes it in
> slurred syllables. jumps up and down and stomps
> his foot and laughs at the cleverness of his ability
> to say what he feels yet disguise it sufficiently
> to keep his words & his envy from hurting himself

Pyorrhead propagandaed pussy profits

> those women who move elegantly as shadows
> in the wake of their white sisters, compulsively
> aping the ways of a culture that excludes them
> while the desire to escape the meanness of their
> vulgar imitations burns through cathode & hearts

Bluehued bluelit blueballs bluetitty blue

> the angst extolled becomes a way of violence
> as much as it is a way of bemoaning the
> inevitable nature of ongoing cultural expulsion
> and subcultural extinction as rape and sodomy
> become extreme expressions of political protest

Frenzied white nationalism muphuckers

> liberation is a state of being within the mind of
> a state—and its like-skinned constituents, no
> matter how demeaned damaged damned still may
> find redress and fair play options in the scheme
> of dreams whereas all others have chances slim-to-zip

Overexposed grinning jonessouled celebs

> those who speak softly of dignity have grown fat-
> tongued, a comfortable minority within a minority
> stoppering the Vesuvius of rage that threatens
> to permanently alter traditional discourse on race
> progress, advancement, and dysassimilation

Dissatisfied cullard chinbottom byrd curses

> if access is circumscribed, likewise is escape
> the means determined by the breadth of one's
> pockets, luck and the generosity of mentors (or
> in that stead, the laziness of overseers) so that
> behind the shroud of one's art might be the door

The African beneath the American

i speak like Plath after the oven did its job

these lines etched in slave-charred flesh
spoken crisply from noose-thickened lips

not a portrait, but a seared rendering
song forced through the throat that fights closing
gasps too painful to contain sentiment

like a smashed stolen grail under centuries of tarnish.

i write on my body. messages for seers.
nakedness as unconventional as foreign as
armed combat with enemies on these shores.

i strive because i must. i love out of spite. i pledge
my allegiance to a standard of ashes, embers, and soot.
this is my anthem, a strident jig in the night

to that music beyond jazz

Faruk Yellow

smudged. about plantation planet
about jazz head jazz,
from ballroom to black bottom
chicken wings between sets
about now, past tense and future

migrational flow across the street
smudged. at Kennedy & Johnson
the appropriation of dream catchers
and kinte cloth by boutique owners
and baldheaded beard eaters

suck dis suck dat
about blond and fuchsia
berets and fro forks giving birth to
(smudged) iambic spastics who
speak in Hopalong Cassidy
and do the can't-dance tango
movin' like a flat pharaoh with a
pyramid up the ying-yang

crass and classless with a bite
of stone nigger, polarized in every
way possible, evicted from
the throne—toilet paper and all
as the ghetto is regentrified by
dot.communists, imitation white with good hair
return with a vengeance

smudged. about inner justice, unity crap
the true black man being snatched out
of his skin by his bicultural twin
rekilled in case there is Ultimate Justice
about fools shooting in despair—dice before bullets

Revisiting Fear and Memphis

we gather in that place that speaks the having-been
of civil war of uncivil assassination

sons named Osceola, daughters named Sojourner

marble monuments gleaned at twilight cast shade
across cold land, river to river, woman, child and man
dedicated to the memory of the murdered
damnable history exhumed by candlelight, etched
on the scroll of martyrdom, the names of the butchered,
the diseased, the lynched and the starved—perished
in the name of race arrogance that they may ascend to those
heavenly lanes lined with Magnolias and stars
no longer the dreamers but The Dream recalled on holidays
when births are celebrated, and the justice not yet
received summoned sorely by weary-lipped prayer

whosoever put their blood in this soil, raise thy standard

White Wall Syndrome—A Study

a)

i sit here like a wound and weep
(a raw treatise on the release of shestuff?)
our accounts are maxed and there is no
assurance that we'll best the odds. nothing
guaranteed as we dance the rim of the brink.
i pay dues to craft organizations that
cannot guarantee me work
or recognition. i belong to the legions
of the heartsick who have no place to
take their grief, core organs dammed,
resenting ambiguous talk of a future

b)

i wonder when so-called friends
don't respond to letters, or return
calls. perhaps they have tired of my
chronic ravings, regard me as a persistent
dreamer and believer in an essential
but unobtainable good—perhaps view me
as an avant-garde hoodoo woman, casting
spells that entangle cumfreaks & Ur-chasers

c)

periodically, i recall the kisses of a man lost to me
whose lips were as thick and intoxicating
as the glue he sniffed. i see him now, hippling
the avenue, across the tracks, an elongated S
curved into the night, huge hand grasping that
stubby brown bag wrinkled at the crown,
as he dangled, nose down, tickled in the poison
that scrambled his words and, likewise, my heart

d)

when i am by myself, i notice that something
inside is dead. i am attempting resurrection

e)

the sheetrock has eyes that follow me
everywhere i go, to the kitchen, to the bathroom
where i take long soaks and scrub
my brownness raw with green soap
and mint leaves in late winter afternoons. they
peer from the bedroom's whiteness
watch me moan under his attentions
which i've done for many years—now,
spying as he spills his happiness into
my willful devotion. and later—as we snore—
pry into our love-spent swoons

f)

i don't want to fuck anyone but him—now

g)

he is of Jupiter. he thrives on enormity. he crushes
the small hopeful things that come within his orbit.
the satellites trapped and circling are coldly inhospitable.
but i know rivers of hot sulfur course beneath his
rainbow-hued crust of storms. that life, while bearing
no resemblance to how i have preferred it, exists
within this thorny creature of traumas and scars

h)

his face, beard and all, charges my softness with devilish radiance

Lorde Cento

i have heard the old spirits chatter

passing black men on the street
who are as if dead (having survived none of the
liberations). let their journey be free of ghosts.

we shall walk as fast as we can
moving beyond anger or failure. we are
rewarded by journeys. we are always saying
goodbye. warning winds will announce us.

hear. hear my heart's voice as it darkens
louder than mourning. the time of
lamentation & curses is passing

somewhere,
in that landscape past noon,

we made strong poems for each other

The Woman in the Mirror

thoughts about rude limousine drivers and cabbies
who do not open doors for me (or turn on the music i want)
and how that corresponds to the rest of the slammed
doors. corridors of them five decades long
wood and iron as tightly bolted, cold as the gravedigger's dick

blinking and squinting with increased
frequency, particularly when working at the monitor
or studying the human face. half-seen ghosts
appear on the edges of catnaps and confusions
there is a special kind of twilight
that inhabits the flesh of the fatigued.

father taught me how to make fire with flint and slate,
to use dried twigs, or a twig and stone, a few dead leaves
he taught me the language of skunks and how to
rid myself of the stench with tomato juice. father taught me
how to pitch a tent, ride a bike, hit a home run. he taught
me that grief grows on the north side of the soul

(the face in the mirror is the face i share with her. contrary
to what others see, i know how narrow & stupid its beauty
can be, not generous at all, frightened and inappropriately
girlish, brazen, and unashamedly lusty)

mother taught me how to take hot plates fresh from
the oven with bare hands. she used to warm
them on the upper rack explaining how rich white people
do not like their food served cold. it was something
i needed to know in case there were no towels handy or if
i unluckily had a hateful boss cook like she'd once had

my sister my girlfriends my bleedings of blood
still my gender my skirts spotted with red after sitting
on the bus or on the car seat the skin between
my thighs so delicate it is torn away by the stickum
the puffy cheeks of a medieval priestess burning her
kinky hair on the altar, burning his broken eggs

blinking and squinting with intensified work-mode
agendas and short-term goal lists taped to keyboards, calendars,
and walls. the priorities are a generation deep and the
notion of meeting them far-fetched. yet, i harvest the mold,
collect the dust and ashes, carry water from deep wells
and damn whatever bone whatever muscle groans

Darwinian Ebb

what was there to begin with

nature in the foreground/unseen things sensed
resistance, therefore, without doubt
a scene where demonstrable horror is linked
to a minimum of means, the glimpse of a shadow
something seen but unrecognizable
in its imposing intimacy

out beyond Orion or encased at the onionlike core
of the self examining itself

one existing without the other yet in perfect if immaterial
correlation/lyricism unleashed and fragmentary
spotting of the skin/psyche/a form dissolving as it travels
room to room, breast to breast

vision recreating vision—the shapelessness of change
metamorphosis comes
reaching toward the whole imagined
a broken entirety.

how much of the future is missing?

whose past is found
in that simple black stone on the sand?

seeing with the heart keeps
form out of character, preserves
the image in the light—divides
this moment from that ancient wholeness

in which we were captured in the margins
and breathed one breath

III.

TWO FUGUES
& A PRAYER

Night Widow Fugue

for in the light the lightness takes

the white shock of sun reveals a loveless vista
sea gulls & ravens compete for discards
then scrape the cloudfree sky

who was here
a moment ago?

loud & noisy
the skin of twenty stayed tough
hung tight and rock & rolled forevah
it has been shed. the shedding, groans & moans & saxophones
no joy in discovering the world was nevah hers

daring frantic drives, subcity spins
burnings

(afterwards, she turns one way
he turns the other)

Ur city catches gold
foreign names & exotic tragedies
compete for headlines & thinning dimes

        have my baby for me
        what?
        you heard me.
        are you serious?
        let's make a baby.
        (silence)
        okay.

outside the windowpane
gnarled branches claw the blue
on impulse something disappears into a bush
there's a distant clang of metal on metal
the bleeding honks of minor Gabriels
sufficient evidence of urbanization

                              when everything happens for the best
                              whose best does it happen for?

            my cold days long on the lard
            short on comfort

o what o what did the blind thief steal?

            dandelions

        fear is the small price paid for
        safety & sovereignty
        (the uprising on the urban plantation
        is daddy's nasty ol' secret)
        a virgin English stands in the mirror,
        brushes its maiden hair, achieves
        ecstasy by candlelight
        one hundred strokes and
        not a mark on flawless reflection
        mistakes transformed into miracles of lace,
        madnesses into property settlements

    whereas

        ugly gal she so ugly whupped ugly
        she look in da mirror it crack 'n' shatter
        so she never able to see huhself
        good. her fam'ly tryta be kind
        but dey too honest in dey eyes

'round da house dey start hidin' anythang
give off reflection tryin' ta spare her da shame
special made, hard workin'
she easy to stroke cuz strokin' come rare
she glow in the dark like a candle
don't own nuthin' but ugly

and all extremes of tones in between

he wants to know
"do you feel it?"

how much romance & how many Romeos prove a woman a woman?

she is a mystic statistic
mama. she gives birth
without a man to imperfect
children who carry keys
around their necks. an
extremely rare condition
but there is proof conclusive
beyond normal limits. these
throbbing embryos conceived
after having escaped natural
abortion to develop within
her consciousness sans
fertilization by male, and
though defective they are no
less sensitive. she nurses
them in rare & tender luster

her love a shout her sex a dun

"my wife," he complains,
"she says she loves
me, and i love her but

we have a problem.
she says she can't feel it.
i want to know if you can feel it"

face-up in duskiness
obsessed with devilish machines
this truth is an unnatural thang. this
truth is mean. it enflames. is ordeal
is unattainable perfection
          stone minds & paper-lantern hearts
death is truth is death
          all life & law, a mechanistic construct

          "my wife," he complains,
          "she says she loves me,
          and i love her but she says
          she can't feel it. i want to
          know if you can . . ."

he cries at her knees, so handsome yet
trapped in the myth of The Oversexed Black Man
his prowess assumed, demanded by believers
demanded by his disappointed wife

          "we married as virgins,
          never marry as a virgin."

her ruth, if embraced by the world, would
bring down the silent glacial truth she loathes
yet needs, her spot in it
forced to dwell in the slum of her faith

          over and over again
          he asks her, "do you feel it?"

she would answer,
"i feel what is felt when
touched. it enters and stays.
i know without knowing
how i know."

truth is:
"no, i cannot feel you.
i want to feel you.
but i can't. you're too small
and too narrow"
the unutterably true

she estimates & weighs. is a confession of ineffectiveness
more devastating than a blameless impotence?

so she lies:
"yes, i can feel you.
yes, it feels good."

light light

it occurs to her that his truth
may be very useful, that perhaps he
has learned to tell it for instant sympathy
and sexual gain, to test and arouse as many
women as he wants while on the job—his subtext
his search for his perfect fit. the fact may be the truth,
but as the truth does it serve his lie?

if i dare kneel my tongue would spill
(everybody talks about the smell, not the taste)

i'm a mean lovin' woman
i'll nevah do you wrong

silence sets
in/first—spontaneous
burst of flame
he tells the wife
he is true as
he betrays her
in his search
for the perfect
velvet tightness

when the fit is righteous snug
will he stop the lies and leave her?
as certainly he will leave his lying lover

> when i woke this morning what'd i see?
> 99 miseries stroking at me.

to think one is liberated by birth
to resuscitate lost spirit
to adventure for gold
to trash another country
to chew kava & dance naked
to love the dark where it is easier to feel superior
    among the less sophisticated
    to loll sun-baked in too much green too much rum

high off the boo-tay

but what does the blind man steal?

her pay-as-you-go honesty has had
its price and her hope has written checks all
over town which her behind can't cash
and the bounce is relentless reverb

the rant of one trashed

this life of fewer chances costs more & more to
maintain i hate all i see that reminds me of what
i can't attain. life is mean for a denizen under
rock (cool existence) having things associated
with luxury/life of Mr. Have. i resent you the
better you are the worse off i am. if you offer
me a drink i will swill it down and still claim
thirst. if you offer to buy food i will order the
most expensive thing on the menu and disdain it.
or i might vomit in your plate. if you invite me
into your home i will wreck it with glee

to bump heads
to always do the latest do
to exchange gossip in galleries
to dabble
to sink oneself into an artful stupor
to be reclusive
to masturbate because interpersonal relationships are
      too taxing
to have earth-shaking luck
to become failed yet trendy
to be cavalier with riches paid for in another's blood
to eat opium on love's horizon

you so good sugar
      you so damned good
you so good sugar
      your kisses give me diabetes
you so good sugar
      you piss sweet water
you so good sugar
      i eat that shit every time

⁘

telling fortunes on the side
drew extra cash. all those
gold & silver rings financed
by the afterlife. the child was
enchanted and held her virgin
breath between Mama's visits
to Margo's din of aromatic
mystery, vials glistened,
incense burned and heavy rose
drapes wrung the romance
out of ghosts. she'd never
seen so much jewelry on
so few fingers, such lovely
long mocha hands, nails
lacquered in bronze, blinded
the child with visions of
opal amber & jade, her
semi-straight hair wrapped
in stylish turbans, cobra-thick
braid snaking halfway
down her back, full-chested
& bristling with all-knowing

"your paternal grandmother was a seer," said the Gypsy,
"and you have her eyes."

⁘

    cuidado! perro bravo
    (how viciousness is spelled)

    to make it mean, put ground pepper in its food
        (the first time is observation)

to make it mean, put gunpowder in its food
          (the second is emphasis)
to make it mean, spit
          (the third, a complaint)

gotta light?

                    when i run out of steam, i help myself to
                      a scream on sugar salt & caffeine

missing: a lit cigarette
              one purse
              one future imagined
              several pieces of junk jewelry

i pull my jacket snug around me. i came in
from the streets to find myself in the streets.
with deliberation, friend i think of you reflecting
on things beyond possession knowing that to have
i must steal must risk imprisonment or death
at the hands of my victim made public. i know
the day approaches when i must act before this train
drives me through plate glass and so to bleed in your
ear (your eye if you offer it) eases the pressure
somewhat as i drink my bitterness with the foam
and my embarrassment melts into a muddled
complacency and i'm less the killer, slain by my wit
aroused and my wit which refuses to fold. and if not
fully slain, then blinded and tapping gleefully toward
eventful wakefulness. and what shall i steal now
that i can no longer see, friend?

the news reads of nothing unanticipated
and she absorbs it calmly, her left foot
tapping softly against the permanently stained
white linoleum, discovers the obituary of one long lost

services set for jazz notable
will be held on a month of
Saturdays at the mortuary on
Sugar Hill. he died in seven
agonies on moleskin Monday
while hospitalized for the double
pneumonia he came down with
on his day job which barely paid
the rent on his substandard
digs. birthed in Boston in
Chicago in Cleveland in Cuba in
Detroit in Kansas City in Harlem
in Los Angeles in Louisville
in Little Rock in Memphis in
Natchez in New Orleans in
Philadelphia in San Francisco in
St. Louis in Winnetka, he set
national consciousness ablaze
when he signed on the dotted
red line, that or face eternity
untested untried and unsung

known for all the powerful
feeling he put into his music

and she has neither the time nor dime to send flowers or a note

dementia pugilistica

a quilled succulent, dangerous & lush
untouchable, to be admired for its particular beauty
does well in the sun, requires minimum care

when nothing happens to the good,
dare one devil, 99 more.

so down & desperate
one trauma follows another
is born of the other in the tick of divine anguish
to reconnect, she dials the number for recorded time
even an inhuman voice will do
even the automatic will do
the pretense of a listener in the absence of a listener
better than that peening silence

the next move, prowler? careful this time. take it easy. do not
stumble. next move by noon. quarters. chink chink into the cup.
a burp the equivalent of thank you. on the eve of another breakthru
or break-in? that place mid-forehead, between the eyes.
that spot that distorts time. that question itching at my lids

> *i'm a mean lovin' woman*
> *i won't do you no harm*
> *i'm a mean lovin' woman*
> *i'd love to keep you warm*
> *i'm a mean lovin' woman, baby*
> *all i want to do is keep you warm*

staghunter pretends
to have a reason to rise in the mornings

> raw & crazed
> the opiate of faded roses
> a knot of tongues
> greed on top of greed
> thunderclaps
> urgent fingers

(there's a crack in my head. the screws are too tight. i can't make it alone.)

damn the eyes.
this blind man sees through his skin

missing: two lashes lowered & raised
                    in a sweep of excitement
              one set of red lip prints
              a case of primal stink
              the shakings down in the shoes
              jazz guitar strummings
              ankles hugging ears
              a moist & forgiving noise

eight-thirty
after dinner her lover imagined
compliments her on the fine meal
the heart-warm table prepared
at her wifely pleasure despite
a full sweat on the job
eight-thirty
and his voice is an attitude
with no distinct features
he is a feeling, an abstraction
who exudes nearness tinged
with aftershave & tobacco, his smile
nearly tangible
she senses his shadowy hand firm
around the tumbler, lifting
it to full lips,
downing the sweet punch, ice cubes
half-melted resettle to mark
the end of an instant treasured just after
eight-thirty
as he calls her darlin' or honey pot or
sweetmeat, rising from the chair
gives her that peck
imagined so well on her lips at
eight-thirty
a little business with the boys
and he'll join her in bed around ten

a well-imagined pat on her hips/the radio coming
to life transforms chores into meditation
simply a cozy ritual
imagined at eight-thirty
vanishes at eight-thirty-one with the clatter
of a fork against dirty white linoleum
while the very real children
sit in front of the television set and
the one plate on the table
contains what is left over—cold greasy and uneaten

damn, lady, you've had it rough!
i'm a survivor. so far.
you are testimony to the resilience of The Strong Black
Woman.
i'd rather be rich than resilient.
it appears you've returned home.
i never left home.
what price have you paid?
i'm still paying dues i'd rather not
how much of your soul was bartered?
all of it.
how deep are the scars that never heal?
the scars are to the root.
i am afraid to know.
in your fear resides wisdom.

when in the light the light commands the view

she's a mean lovin' woman
her love is never done

every blow dealt is a pinched nerve felt

"but do you feel me?"

she's a mean lovin' woman
baby, she don't mean no harm

she rises with the sun, sleeps on the run

missing: one escape route

root animal, eyes rove, collared
avenues dim-lit and distant
with stark, singular deliberation—a black
& hungry leatherette studded in blood-red
brads, forks over all available skins.
this is an act of art/tongues tangled all that
wet stinky coiled crotch hair root for root's sake,
spent licky fingers bone in the teeth, tastes
so hot & terrible

(as if a reason is needed "just because" you say)

rest follows the pill. inside cool air circulates
by the plastic blade of a drugstore fan.
they are at rest between making mysteries

eyes shaded, shadowed. curved inward toward
his groin, her buttocks, promontories with
which he loves to smother himself until
he's slick & wet. she's lovely & large and it's
so easy to find one's way into her kindness
looking at her in the radiance, watching it etch
his likeness across her earth-toned breasts
nipples sucked swollen like olives, his fingers
collect below her navel like tickle spiders

toward that perfect ensoulment

love weather. two goblets of wine,
a joint. yellow lace under starlight.
kisses wild & electric. graceful fucking

        very soon
        you must try it, if not now
        two moves from now.
        today there is everything between us
        i've made this fantasy just for you

for in the light the lightness takes its due

Sorceress of Muntu

raven lips & red tongue rhythming forth deluge

backcity haunts
rise out of clouds of confusion
walls stippled in a militant ogham

                 feeler to feelee

certainly she has spooked this turf before
discovered feasts laid out for the taking
sacrifice fit for a blues goddess
his offering, the long cool drink of his body
the rhyme of his gift to embitter
the harmonics of a bopking going down slow

      been down to the welfare
      down to the union hall
      been down to the welfare
      down to the union hall
      those bureaucrats done got me
      gonna cancel out the call

temptation in the sheen of glossy magazine covers
in the sweat of kliegs Hollywood-style burning moths by the ton

(what was wanted was a smooch what was got was a problem)

      been down to the welfare
      down to the union hall
      been down to the welfare
      down to the union hall
      don't call me no account, lover
      creepin' fast as i can crawl

a pernicious melody & cruel mockish bass line
muddies the high of sunblessed southwestern afternoons

a lunar wedge skittering on the rim of sleep's rise
every dreamer a fool, every fool flyin'

ladybug ladybug where have you been?

    too generous a giver
    she gives herself away

    remember that Senegal gal? she married a holler
    & he promptly stole her educated tongue

    she vowed she would not rest till happiness
    climbed out of the abyss by its bloody paws

    her words died during fever

in bondage to contentment, sprawled across the sofa
legs akimbo, belly-to-belly, raising dust & hallelujahs

once born
    taste the blood
twice born
    taste the brew
thrice born
    taste the spirit

the thought of being mistaken for an authentic
(rub up & down, rub up & down) titillates

            nomen dubium

    looking up the nose, a dream
    can become a snotdrop

can become bubble gum sticking
to one's aspirations
can become the oil-slicked front tires
hit-a-skid as the car careens off
the road eliciting screams for
God & insurance agents

jes a jitterbug everywhere she go

crossover & comeback costs mightily with each passage
only so many trips to be made fo' weakness sets in
worst thang is gettin' stranded twixt will & won't

> (the metaphysics of denial/graves
> into suppositions of graves. once
> ambiguity is established there's
> zip budget for gratitude)

what came in on soft-spoken croon & a smile
was nowhere near the information needed let alone required
what sat down, crossed its legs, & made with the welcome
was concealing the best hidden in places beyond obvious reach
what played kissyface with the future
      was milking the past for profit
& also
took advantage of the ravenous by offering a lunch of tough crust
while the fruitful filling was retained for true pie later
the wisdom finger pointed knowingly in error
sending the zany bunch galloping toward capture
what came in & sat for a brief & pleasing spell
was studying the mark, mapping the dupe

yo ignorati

it was gotten wrong cuz it was given wrong

street stupid

preoccupied with the game of the moment
missing out on the game of a lifetime

       the connoisseur of black history
       reads it cover to cover
       except when she gets to the nasty parts
       then she flips the pages

baptism by ballot
bride to the backhand
hittin' the bricks after a breakfast
of grits & hardtack
clothed in rags 'n' bustin' out at the nates
one-two one-two baptism by fist
jealousy geechie-style
sucker-punched red as a Rex lard bucket
got more hump than a camel
wouldn't cross the street for one of her smiles
yet voiceless & choiceless
aiming to settle all the scores in a
baptism by bullet

like black Athena rising whole from godhead

lo street mystic weaver of spells from autumn nights
& crème de menthe, transformer of cotton into lamé,
street lamps into bonfires, aches into bliss

          no pretty today
          no sweet
          no pretty today
          no good to eat

he say he hates me yet don't see me die in his eyes

                    no pretty
                    today no sweet
                    no pretty today
                    what i eat

something aromatic & high-caloric always
on the back burner—a riot of rind, fat molecules, & onions

          whatevah happened to Monte X
          who loved the truth until it paid him a visit?
          did he discover hell is a condition of access? that
          power imagined fails in the lap of power actualized?
          (his peculiar allergy being an intolerance to anything
          tight at his neck, his having been lynched in a former life)

          whatevah happened to Monte X who
          loved the revolution even after its nuts were busted?
          did he impale himself on his ultrashit natural fork?
          or overdose on rhythm-and-dues agitprop?

          whatevah happened to Monte X who
          brought down the tzar of The Word Factory?
          did he drown in the tsunami of reader complacency?
          or in the ejaculatory smugness of neo-Tom lovecoons?

too cute to move

          X, sugar
          how is it, now, that you have the freedom
          to host a TV talk show, drink Chivas Regal neat, drive
          an imported Italian pimpmobile & die a landlord?

some incisors some oak bark some burnt lemon tea
a tome chock-full of unremarkable things like
the death of angry days & the nights of sorry life,
one or two sweet daddies & some burgundy hose.

Mecca's now a shopping mall & the used-to-be cock
of soulfire spends Sunday afternoons being ignored at
book signings, buffing his nails, knocking the dust
off his nines, waiting for the invaders who promised
they were coming, but by subway instead of cab

some bug jigglin' earphonics

                                        so what residual slavery?
                            all those couchy niggahs wants is
                                their share of the plantation.
        dig it, X
        still waiting for the war that did not come
        still sleeping with one eye open & one hand
        over the butthole

        Mr. X if you can hear this wiggle your niggahtoes

        oh my Mr. X what a big Bedouin horn you blow

skibbledeebibbledeeboo
wahzoo wahzeh wahzoo

o tragic muse

where oh where are those smiling pom-pom waving
empathizers when you need them?

                        how does one cope when born against one's will?
o tragic muse

does excessive grease applied to the grill
guarantee a richer fire?

                        do the rocks cry out when they strike heads silly?
o tragic muse

aren't you the one with skin so black & thick
so devoid of human pathos even bruises don't show?

                              how many Washingtons does it take to buy the lie?
o tragic muse

who made furniture from all that moral redwood
protecting the esprit de corps from erosion?

                              does one who sucks face die of distention?
o tragic muse

who slew the Loop Hoodoo after a cleverly placed Ghede bug
revealed his enormous whereabouts?

                    the dopekillers don't use bad words,
                    they believe in curses
                    the dopekillers are full of absolutes by which
                    they circumscribe prey
                    the dopekillers have soft soles
                    the dopekillers know clean money is a myth

one thousand carphones infiltrate the penitentiary
each with an urban youth inside
(jes another interchangeable part to fill
some bugger's spurious agenda)
hidden in cases of frozen hamburger meat
labeled "Fuck Ups"
one thousand wardens, each with a state budget
& a small town's economy at stake, move in

starved for The Getaway

              amulets, talismans, warders-off

                              woke up on the wrong side
                              of self-restraint this morning

buggin'

each day a needed conjure
a chant to prevent pregnancy or draw money
invisibility powder cloaks dirty deeds
right root dispels deep dumps a potion sustains love's erection
& a foul-smelling goo turns black to white
without altering hair

gators boarding nighttrains digging
nighthawks doing the nightcrawl in their nighties
in a northerly direction

                              say whose laziness is sloth
                                    whose resistance?

            leader leader who got the leader?
            can we get the news from Cleveland
            or do we have to wait on Super-U-Spook?
            is he still into that Noxzema thang
            or did he graduate to Oil of Ofay?

something gray's creeping across liberty's
consciousness/the psychobabble of late video decline
a savage & wasteful piece of fiction
like Usher splurping into the primordial sludge
evidence of the dyspeptic generation
ancient rockers enshrined in leather,
an overground of causeless rebels glassed out
of upper corporate echelons

(select geldings & thoroughbreds hang in the winners' circle
no dray horses no mavericks allowed)

                        this our governance of bitter wills holding up
                            the rune-riddled corpse that walks & hates

like bugs up the bongalong

daffy if only you knew

an awareness of linguistic nuances poses a
prose slightly less involuted than usual
yet indigestible, meaning the encounter
between concrete & sublime is inevitable
& inevitably complex. there being
no eschatological solution to this deep chaos.
false hopes abound as a measure to sustain
the hopeless in going to a presaged doom

        (somethin' made for lovin' in the radar oven)

controversy meaning big box-office
it takes exorbitant memberships
in private pleasure palaces
it takes dealers impervious to busts
it takes a mature & pandemic trust
lacking that it's the feathers of public education
(what good does it do to excel?)
the hysterectomy of the woman politic
without sufficient symptomatology
surface on surface in surface
a social cervixation resulting in
excess criminal justice studies by
malnourished & undersexed academics
& the imprisonment of mothers who
inadequately breast-feed causing
the bloating & nausea indicative of
future adults addicted to riverboat
gambling, 80-proof pabulum & Cuban cigars

    lookylooky here comes the master p
    gotta big hat gotta big hair, say

one night i was hittin' the pipe, cruising out
then coming in alone, a violin concerto
all in my parts
& some rude bird in a beret
with a fat orange ass feather came peckin'
at my boudoir door chirpin'
"Ramona"
i broke loose for the closet & honored
his intrusion with my best pair of
brogans upside his noggin

speak yo squeak o master p
smart whiskers & four eyes
gotta laid-back pose with sandaled feet
does baptism by leak
when the master raps evahbody eats

something aromatic promising a salacious & well-savored demise

they shootin' up Miles again shitfaced
in the east. up north they're still
free basin' Miles. growin' big bushy blue
buds of Miles high in the south. out
west they cut Miles with a little
Mingus & positively ruin theyselves

what does one do when in the court of public opinion
all one's objections are overruled? all escape
routes cemented over

babee, ain't no crime to like saltines with your soup
or peanut butter with your grahams

(the gypsy shook her crystal ball. they
watched the future settle like synthetic snowflakes. she

bucked her eyes, rubbed them, looked again
then hissed. "seems your hip white girlfriends can't
hold their alcohol & always die on you.")

Hespere

once upon a dream there was a dark queen who ruled a
demiworld beyond knowing. there she lived unhappily in
her dreary palace entombed by the love that fathered her.
the gems in her crown were simple stones, her
raiment crude & ill-fitting, her hair a nest of
brambles. all she possessed was of shade or covered
in rainbow-colored moss. there she thrived in volcanic
radiance & iridescent splendor yet she pined for
another world made steel by her false imaginings & in
the pitch of her moonless golden-appled grove she danced
her dissatisfactions amongst ghosts

abyssus abyssum invocat

for the longest time she assumes they
don't know what they're doing to her

she is convinced she can somehow
explain it to them they'll understand &

(if it didn't happen to them it didn't happen)

their attitudes will change when that
doesn't occur she assumes blame/it's her

failing/her inability to express herself
adequately & she searches/seeks the means of

(if it happened it's minor or exaggerated)
mi furia no es su furia

meaning to make her displeasure
irrevocably appreciated & then during

some trauma she realizes they've understood
all along they've anticipated her

       (having had so little what's a little less

       bills bills i'm up to my gills
       here my sistuh here my brutha
       here's one chunk here's another
       you too mutha?)

every scamper. it didn't matter how
poor or how exquisite her blatherings

her image was clear in the unexposed
depths without her hamsterings to impart

her specialized differentiation it was
intended she should suffer

(experience is too relative to be relevant)
my holocaust is not your holocaust

her communication of that suffering only reassured
& confirmed their success & the effectiveness

of their strategies. & so with this knowing

          (contemplation is superior to interaction)

she's damned/was damned from conception
her frayed wishbook filthy with thumbstains
her damnation her life's art & hahahahaha

her emesis an entertainment

she tells of the dead who stretch their arms
to prod. they whisper loud disenchantments. they send
mushrooms & clover. they become itches in
unspeakable places at embarrassing moments. they
nest in afterthots & slam windows unexpectedly

                    extraña vida de los colores

night widow the trance broken
a muted & narcoleptic residual chalks her lips
the phone rings, night widow
answers it through her silence her distance
hears the exasperated hiss & whisper
his hang up/the dial tone
cradles the receiver & takes note of the clock
waits for him to fill her with his
grease monkey experience. he fights
his addiction to love her but he's not
himself. she loves him to life. he's creepin'
as fast as he can crawl

night widow, sleepless, suspended
between lust & numbness
caught without comfort, she holds
herself by her own elbows, as unchained
monsters gurgle & clatter in her
bowels as do imagined probabilities
a blues pilgrimage to Chicago pending

a blacker disposition/violence stillborn
stress attacks. stalled. shooting brains

night widow on that thottrain circling her pillow
equal parts water & grim believer

betrayed by Levolor blinds, head throbbing
eyes squinting. someone forgot to turn off the blues

> *it comes down to breathing*
> *sometimes honey*
> *it's easy to talk of love*
> *when you're fat money*
> *& a day's hard sweat has never stank*
> *your armpits honey*

> *i'd love to play*
> *among the roses lover*
> *& have you keep my toes warm,*
> *lover. i'd love to lay down the gun*
> *& call it truce*

he's home from work. she senses him before
she sees him/hatred sizzles the air, disrupts
her hummings. he stands against the doorjamb, chest
heaving, eyes murder space for eternity
then slowly bring her into focus. he slumps
into a chair, reduced to stone-age essential, lips
taut against teeth, nostrils smoldering,
the four walls twitch as does her stomach. she
can't think of anything to say to dispel the
stifling funk. she's afraid to touch him. he's
beyond tired, is whipped & she's trapped
in hurt-widened eyes which suddenly narrow
accompanied by contortions of his tight jaw
& tense fists which open & close to open to
close as he compels her in his stare, slowly parts
his lips into a tortured twist & hisses, "hello."

> *but it comes down to breathing*
> *sometimes honey*

there's fight needin' to be fought
now honey, as much my children's meat
as mine altho more sleep
would be divine

so when the shades are drawn
honey, even a burial
will cost breathin' money
so let 'em fry me & toss me
on the storm

her gift is failed, has lost its effusive
bronze gleam. layers of plating
are peeled back, reveal the worthless tarry vinyl
beneath. a moaning maw oozing hot slime
& eyes & thighs clammed shut

i'd love to play
among the roses lover or pick
the petals from the stem
have you keep my toes warm,
lover. i'd love to lie beside
you in the rain

comes ugly to breathing
sometimes honey, & it's easy
to clown talk honey, when
the stage is yours & you've
never known the art of pain

night widow rising from the wicked pillow
joyfilled
still in the glow of the pearl humming
the movement of his hands in amberlight
the sting of his salt fresh on her bee-stung lips
night widow rising from the joyful pillow

her head bursts with purple flurries
morning glories

backcity haunts
where Nyx descends smartly
sampling the local flavor, guided by raven lips & red tongue
discovers a feast of rhythms laid out for the hearing
a long drink of cool
certainly, she has spooked this turf before
there for the stumbling over

the long procrastination has become habit,
each night prolonged, sunrise delayed,
the stars, veins collapsed, now settle for nebulae
& the dance of visions induced by angels of dust
narcospasms bedevil long-time somnambulists,
threaten repose, exacerbate restlessness
solar disks blazing against the sky on sleep's horizon

every dreamer a fool & every fool flyin'

Prayer for America Reborn

o deep waters breaking. good. wash away

end this soullessness where
weakness is fostered, fed on, yet the weak punished
disproportionately for their weaknesses
where harmless indiscretions are fodder
for the lies of bigots, fascists, and misanthropes
where community is counterfeit

end the reign of the bogus in the name of the correct

let the just go forth

o deep waters rising. mother the good. wash away

end this soullessness where
the hypocrites & heartless in power force an
inhumane asceticism on the powerless
litigate their advocates into ineffectiveness
starve the heartful into meanness. where the worker
is devalued and the different valueless

end the reign of fakery in the name of the pious

let the brave find their fists

o deep waters roiling. father the good. wash away

end this soullessness where
wounded lives fester unhealed and unexpressed
where quality and tenderness are beyond
the means of the needy. where the dysfunctional

are consigned to prisons streets state crematoriums
where cartoon cults console the disarranged

(ever the ravenous devour the earth)

end the reign of callousness in the name of economy
let the lovers go forth

o deep waters rising. manchild the good. wash away

end this soullessness where
entertainment is religion, trickery
and cruelty are legitimized, institutions are
founded on fear, tradition is the calcification
of denial, sincerity a character flaw
where affectation rules over authenticity
end the reign of murderers in the guise of law and order

let the long-silenced speak

o deep waters rising. womanchild the good. wash away

end this soullessness where
the deceitful and the greed-mongers flourish
thugs control the flow of beauty and the artless
control the artful. where abuse for profit
is rewarded where self-censorship is rewarded where
cowardice is rewarded and dark brilliance shunned

o deep water risings. gatherings of the good for the good

end the reign of false prosperity
in the name of progress
end the reign of arrogance
in the name of education

end the reign of denigration
in the name of justice

let the song go forth on spacious skies

o deep water rushings wash good at dawn's gloryrise

IV.

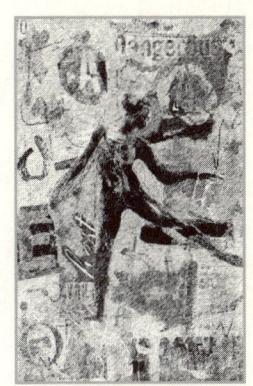

THE WEIGHING OF MY HEART

Fool's Progress

awed awkward and afraid
i am no longer sure, these days, if i'm seeing
straight or crooked or double
i talk to scorpions in my sleep
and visit sites of ancient intrigues

when questioned on hate
i'm an encyclopedia of bruises

when awake i contemplate isolation,
the benefits of self-imposed gratitude
and retirement on the margin of the margin
(as always, mainstream compliance is impossible)
a dearth of out-of-print books
a once played guitar
a collection of first edition nightmares

sometimes i sleepwalk
trapped between a closing and an opening

battered on a Pacifica of angry whisperers
who demand it all, having nothing
but this fury between my ears

by late afternoon my red eyes have cleared
and consciousness is certain, focus
on the present conspiracy is reminiscent
of a muddled past. it is then that
i do my best knifing in the kitchen
where you are welcome any time

behind closed doors
i am reserved and do my secret bleeding

knock twice before you enter

Gone Exits

listen for the sound—echoes, emotions
beneath the surface. it stirs.
i hear Corso whispering "solid"
(he's a conch blower, eats crackling fish)

i wear desperation like a birthmark (it's too late
to die young and too early to die in my sleep)

there for the bold to read—the living is
murder by daylight, romance by night
the psychometrists have failed to measure the
contents of my heart

living on nothing but tea leaves and jeremiads
an unsteady diet for the inky mind. cold explodes

found unconscious and poetically defective

a demagogue crying in the wilderness
lizard-skin wisdom roach-infested ashtrays
shivers and kicks, down to the assbone
searching holy pockets for wayward nickels
a dance to entertain whimpering sycophants
all drowning in the same yacht, noisy and undignified

climbing over the next man's neck
a riot of rhythm and blues rap

love those Ubangi lips those liver lips those ohsokissables
with every beat of my fist

you heard me arrive, mangling your name

Sour Apples

—after Ted Berrigan

i have lived what others have lied about living

time bursts and drifts like a great flatulence
and i am offended as the nation grows stale
the arts and humanities stagnate

the bloodless leading the bloody as culture wars
are renewed/as panderers and profligates
displace working parents and prophets

no songlines or drinking gourds guide me to safety

without normal limits
who fucks and settles into mock serenity
      under these skirts
      is not peaceful by nature

where is my constituency?
what hoodoo must i stomp?
what president must i elect?
what murder must i commit?
what god must i declare dead?

mother. i hate this tarbaby's love of you
and wrench it from my being

the history of my body

a crushed rose
the workings seem obtuse
indigenous harmonies, all glittery
rubble & love blazing white teeth
the portrait of a sunburnt face
dayblooming pickaninnies
exploding hips/*encantados de la luna*
pavement by night
from ashy to bone dry
flying houses and thunder palms
penny-candy memories ·
violent eruptions of beauty
wailing sirens into the deep pink
just a dream of cities
ample-voiced harbinger
mouth made for sloppy kisses
(goodness gracious she's bodacious)
question mark, forever haunted
tenderly fiercely fleshed

Slave Driven

i barely niggle a living squirreling around
the home office. i work for myself as my own secretary.
it's a shitty job, paperwork ceiling to floor. the
technology changes every few months. i'm on call
weekends and holidays. no benefits or perks.
there's no vacation or overtime. the pay is less
      than minimum wage.
it's like every job i've ever had except i don't drive
rush-hour traffic and can wear nightclothes if i want.
there are no racist vibes, no gender or sex preference
or intergenerational discrimination. quitting time
is determined by level of exhaustion.
      i get no breaks. i sit all day.
      i grab a bite while on duty
      the boss never has anything
      good to say

Olio Intaglio

they would not let me do what i could have done
these many years for my children
i could not find a safe place because there were
no safe places. i could not heal because there were
no sacrariums sancta in our neighborhood. they kept me
trapped in that spiritless daunting
place. they plagued us day and night, those faceless
phantoms spewing their noxious hate, poisoning
the air the water the ground/our blood
they would not let me be who i was to do what
i could lo these years stolen from my children

my son yearned to be royal/loved royalty
(but you were—as they say—a prince among princes)
in lavender robes and golden slippers,
crowns woven from rolls of soft white tissue.
he created an imaginary dynasty of kings and queens
whose children were not left alone because
mother wasn't beautiful enough or smart enough

they ain't made the dress blacker than my heart

silk holds the spirit, cotton shreds it
(this is the quilt i weave)

i worried that they would kill my children
and then not come for me

one down.

harvesters of hate, what do you gather? those billions
keeping you safe from my fury

the women did not come to sit with me.
my sister did not come. my daughter could
not come (but was excused). my aunts did not visit,
but telephoned. my life-giver, my sustainer, my mother
did not come. their chairs were empty and i sat alone
on hard wood half ice half concrete

cousins, girlfriends, sistuhs. quietly absent
don't speak to me.
we have shared nothing. not even childbirth

tears drop loudly
great splotches

my steps the cadence of a march, now—
the strain is in the making of them all
stand and salute the glory, bitches
the body sags but the soul is strident

sleepless nights, tears, taking on weight like the Titanic
taking on ocean

i sat alone. no one brought food. no one called
not the wives of my brothers. not my nieces

i sat alone on hard wood in the kitchen with the ghosts

had i sown nothing but emptiness and loss?

in a figurative way
always except for
times when—
the dying underground,
he is now submerged in my dreams

i have wrung my heart
in secret silence

i have wailed loud enough
to bring down heaven
but my hurt is ever
the unheralded kind of hurt—
few want to see it or hear about it.
it is not positive, rather it is
too tough to look at squarely
better to look beyond it

i am the nightlight

(before leaving, i would tuck him in gently
under the sheets like when he was newborn)

after his spirit lifted
i took snapshots of his beautiful corpse to remember

to those women, i say your tragedy
is that you did not have a son
like my son. you did not know him
even for a minute. you did not watch
the sun redden his sand-gold hair
after playing outdoors. you did not tell
him bedtime sagas. you did not make
certain he was clean between his toes,
behind his ears and around his belly button.
you did not join his laughter

the voice in my head. the invisible speaks

this is the load i am discharging
until i gather the strength to carry it on

the weight of his no longer being in this world
the image of him

About Our Unborn

we have never made a child
and now we are infertile/have transformed
ourselves. you are an armchair statistician
and i am a chigger-bitten statistic. still
the positives are waiting and waiting
and waiting. (grandtots, daughter, son, & son
all once removed.)
                        we force Apollo across
the smog-blitzed sky every morning
and dare Morpheus to catch us snoring

how much gargantuan effort to secure
the economically correct future?

it is said that our victory will come
          and
that we will roar as we seize it
          and
no one will notice
                    the tremors
                    the stained & broken teeth
                    your slight stoop
                    my crutch

Baptism

riptide washes over
and the depths of oceanic rhythms
correct every effing mistake.
they are not in this room. just the sounds
(the boomshockaboom rattling floorboards)
marginalized—from the left and the right

i am visiting this stereophonic past
because i'm not only thirsty in general
but a bloodthirsty blood

and water equals peace of mind
an unhurried soak in the tub
to sooth the savage in the veins
like a glass of liver-corrupter

the light languor of liquor going to his head and mind
the unpainted nudes—four hundred pounds
of raw do-it-to-me/the same way snakes dance
the noisy passion of lovers full hitch
this is the place in the music where
the soloist steps up to the mike
and obsesses over an ear
and the couches and tables catch fire
and there's a burning
in the thickness

The Museum of You

1)

you have now lived long enough to roam
a room filled with your personal leavings

that was your favorite reading chair
with its ottoman on which you propped your feet

it's difficult to believe that you actually sat
at that sad little desk and did your greatest doings
there. see, the broken drawer's been repaired.
the scratch you made with those old scissors
seems as fresh as the moment you made it. there's
that cigarette burn, and that piece of unremovable tape

2)

so many hours your eyes roved that painting.
you entered it. you went beyond it. it inspired you. it provided escape.
you liked to lean back in your swivel chair
and drink it
in the afternoon light.
you believed there was a psychic connection
between you & the artist

3)

here you are, the perfect likeness
carved in an ebony of rare quality, an abstract nude
the lines of your configuration
fluid & essence-filled

4)

among your artifacts
the hand-painted Australian boomerang

the blue clay owl
the jug of aborted dreams

(you are that forgotten thing
in the basement brought over from Africa,
uncrated and unadmired, sleeping
as you've slept for centuries)

5)

oh, the tour too brief. the docent retires.
you find yourself unexpectedly alone at the exit

you make yourself believe that you
are among the lucky,
having lived long enough to run your finger
through your own dust

The Weighing of My Heart

spading for freedom. down to the roots

i sustain the consequences of foolish acts
done by others, gestures intended to harm me,
the way ocean fills the sinking craft as one bails

"community or cobwebs?" he demands. i hear
the threat. "living i sought the living," i answer.

every wink and ogle paid for.

passing my hand through the space
that should define the heart. aortic cavity. trapped there.
in a heaviness (watch that shimmy, my thighs
disturbing the ether. hear the clap-and-tremble)

i am on stage within minutes pulling back the layers
of my psyche/another tragicomic episode, another misfire

      the i of me/the omymy of mine—*and there she goes*
      on twinkling toes in tore-up queen-sized hose

not in the mode. i can feel the fat
bunching up around my future. the self as
four-poster with too many sag-sorry pillows—
eiderdown and nappy black coils

     claustrophobic mirrors

my pain minimized in a coffin text of
stone—the lovelessness that glosses over the
damage and confines me to the margins.

cobwebs or community?
the answer demeans/makes the difference
twixt? having some and having none

in the realm of the political, choice rules out rebellion

passing my hand along the member that
defines a disappointment. true to my ideals/all
empty pockets and sophisticated syntax
(i haunt his sleep yet dream of my sister
murdered for meager things. a Bible. a stubbornness.
a bad marriage. too much Indian blood)

this isn't the death i dreamed of. who is
this lizard-tongued bedeviler with the ape's amble?
when we touch it's always a cavort on surface

texture. moving. like something hard
through something harder. like dad's belt
buckle or mom's switch. like the
cost-of-loving indicator

dying, i seek the dead.
moving. like leaves in a southwestern briskness
like pampas grass. like trauma to fist

speak to me of lost islands/lives taken by this sea/
white foam and winged scavengers diving for salvage

the looks that no longer come. indifference witnessed

heaven and earth have failed to connect
there is nothing to shield me

is God willing?

sun the fronds sun the plaza sun the sizzle
of denuded flesh sun the vocabulary of smoke
and smolder sun on my knees in the sun

Hap, creator of all things, hear me

i am passing my heart through the wall of resistance
it bursts in my hands, bleeds to the wood

blemished. ash-based soap. rags. cold water

cobwebs and more cobwebs—a community of spiders
and archserpents

i am haunted by the absence contained in an urn
the heat of hormonal ebb/bones weeping calcium & dreams

within the realm of thought, desire rules out randomness

the way of my heart a looking-glass landscape

(i wear the colors of autumn
i smell of ash. i possess the details
of reasonswhynot, pour the rum
and collect the thunder)

give me a golden lyre, a braid of hair
you are my curse. you are my destruction
you take my eyes and make them opals
you take my mouth and make it coral

i must become a keeper of silences
retire to the cell and take meals without salt
the vases of red gladioli intended for another
my nails unpainted, my feet swollen as
circulation slows and girth grows

and there, i will watch from the shadows
a disgruntled sentinel where i await the arrival
of The Final Truth, my eyes blind to all but the glory

spiritless
bedeviled
a murderous
something
moving harder
as it passes

Peace

—for Al in Vietnam 1965

distance is a threat, and time

but i will wait—*hoping*

that bullet kills somebody else
that shrapnel blinds another's eye
that napalmed flesh, not yours
the bayonet-strewn guts, the enemy's

and let the war—all wars
be fought on soft mattresses

between legs and lovers

Passing through the Blood

simply   because you are hungry
       with hot black ink
it doesn't follow that   power rises
those memories are   not yours. deny them.
         everything
must be used: your eyes   your heart
     accept one day
as another. learn   to cherish.   being brave
        no easier
in the morning   whatever you discard
     never mourn
anything wasteful   relive slavery. follow
       the most do-worthy
ever-dreaming is not eternal   defend
     your rainbow
respect whatever   sustains   you. tell them
       your mother   was
a darkness

Exoteric

what is life's purpose?

            change diapers when necessary

how we think about death

            open the window. it's hot in here

what we cling to in the midst of change

            your cold hand. let me warm it

ACKNOWLEDGMENTS

Grateful acknowledgment is made to the editors of the anthologies and magazines where some of these poems previously appeared: *The Antioch Review* ("Baptism"); *The Bomb: The Arts & Culture Quarterly* ("The Museum of You"); *Eclipse: A Literary Journal* ("White Wall Syndrome"); *88: A Journal of Contemporary American Poetry* ("Darwinian Ebb" and "Revisiting Fear and Memphis"); *The Kindred Spirit* ("Meanwhile in San Francisco"); *Little Noir Anthology* on-line ["The Door" at www.lapoetry.com] ("Things Go Sour"); *Nocturnes 2: Review of the Literary Arts* ("The Weighing of My Heart"); *Oxygen* ("Broken Rhythms"); *Poetry New Zealand* ("Night Widow Fugue"); *Prayers for a Thousand Years* ("Prayer for America Reborn"); *The Progressive* ("Soul Traveler"); *Rivendell* ("Los Angeles Nocturne"); *Shattersheet* ("Exoteric"); *wake up heavy* ("A Second Death"); and *Zyzzyva* ("Sorceress of Muntu").

The completion of this manuscript was facilitated by a fellowship in poetry from the California Arts Council, summer/fall 2002. Special thanks to Austin Straus for editorial assistance, and to Ed Ochester for his thoughtfulness, and for asking.

Wanda Coleman has received numerous awards for her poetry and fiction, including a Djerassi residency and fellowships from the John Simon Guggenheim Foundation, the National Endowment for the Arts, and the California Arts Council. She received the 1999 Lenore Marshall Prize for *Bathwater Wine* from the Academy of American Poets, *The Nation*, and the New Hope Foundation. She was a bronze-medal finalist at the 2001 National Book Awards for *Mercurochrome: New Poems*. Ms. Coleman's work has appeared in such anthologies as *The Best American Poetry; The Norton Anthology of African American Literature; Trouble the Water: 250 Years of African American Poetry;* and *The United States of Poetry.* Renowned for her poetry performances, she has sustained herself in a variety of professions, including Emmy award–winning scriptwriter, medical secretary, and teacher at the university level. Born in the Los Angleles community of Watts and raised in South Central, she resides in Southern California.